BADLANDS:
BEAUTY CARVED FROM NATURE

Linda R. Wade

ROURKE ENTERPRISES, INC.
Vero Beach, FL 32964

Library of Congress Cataloging-in-Publication Data

Wade, Linda R.
    Badlands: beauty carved from nature / by Linda R. Wade.
    p. cm. – (Doors to America's past)

    Includes index.
    Summary: Describes the beauty and desolation of the barren region known as the Badlands, the historic events connected with it, and what it is like today.
    ISBN 0-86592-471-6
    1. Badlands National Park (S.D.) – Juvenile literature. 2. Geology – South Dakota – Badlands National Park – Juvenile literature. [1. Badlands National Park (S.D.) 2. National parks and reserves.] I. Title. II. Series: Wade, Linda R. Doors to America's past.
F657.B24W33 1991
508.783'9 – dc20

90-46577
CIP
AC

Acknowledgments

    Special thanks to Chief Naturalist Joe Zarki, and Valerie Naylor, of Badlands National Park, for information and slides; Jay Shuler, former Chief Naturalist of Badlands National Park; Bill Hamm, a Park Interpreter; and Marvene Viis of the South Dakota State Historical Museum, for extensive picture research.

Photo Credits

Courtesy of the Badlands National Park: 35 (right) by Paul Horstead, 37 (right) by Jay Shuler
Courtesy of the South Dakota State Historical Museum: 21, 23, 25
Rushmore Photo, Inc.: cover, 1, 5, 8, 10, 13, 30, 32, 33, 34, 35 (left), 37 (left), 41, 42, 45
South Dakota State Historical Society, Courtesy of Smithsonian Institution: 17, 20

Table of Contents

Introduction

Nestled in the southwest corner of South Dakota is a region that is both starkly barren and remarkably beautiful. Called the Badlands, the area was carved out through ages of natural erosion. Millions of years of wind, water, and frost have cut through layers of mud, clay, gravel, limestone, and other rock to create this fascinating world.

In places, the Badlands appear almost to be the ruins of an ancient city. The striking landscape displays sawtoothed spires of rock rising into the sky, deep gorges and gullies, steep hills and ridges, high-walled cliffs and canyons, pointy pyramids and rounded mounds, massive grassy-topped buttes, and castlelike formations of stone with various colors streaked across them. Yet, no list of features can fairly describe the Badlands. Perhaps it is simplest to say only that here nature has carved out an astonishing sculpture unlike any other on Earth.

The Badlands have long intrigued—and challenged—people. Outlaws in frontier days occasionally tried to hide in this desolate and fantastically carved land, but even they didn't stay long. For along with the Badlands' haunting beauty come temperatures that can be extreme, and good water is not easily found there. Only muddy or

Formations show erosion.

white rivers and streams flow through the area. Their waters are not suitable for drinking.

The name *badlands* came from the Native Americans who lived in the area in the 1700s. They referred to it as *mako sica*, which means "land bad," in the sense of "rough." And French-Canadian fur trappers who explored the area called it, in their native tongue, *les mauvaises terres à traverser*. That means "bad lands to travel across."

Today, we know the place simply as the Badlands. But the name has come to describe far more than the severe and scenic landscape of the area. The name also announces the enormous geologic wealth of the place. The Badlands are one of the Earth's richest fossil beds. Fossils are the remains of plants and animals preserved in rock. The Badlands contain the Earth's best-known remains of land mammals that date back 35 million years.

In addition to being a place of scenic wonder and geologic value, the Badlands also are a remnant of one of the world's largest grasslands. Scattered among the unusual rock formations are grassy expanses, sometimes covering small areas, sometimes large. For the Badlands are located on the vast flat, treeless plains that cover the entire central portion of the United States. These plains sometimes are called the prairie. More than 60 percent of the Badlands are made up of outstanding mixed-grass prairie.

Scenic marvel, geologic wonder, remnant of the vanishing American prairie—these are the Badlands. Let's visit this ancient and awesome corner of the United States.

1

What Are Badlands?

The word badlands can be used in two ways. In its widest sense, the word describes any area where severe water and wind erosion have created small hills and gullies, often in colorful and bizarre shapes. A badlands area usually also has a semi-arid, or fairly dry, climate. The infrequent but torrential downpours of rain in such areas speed up the weathering, or wearing away, of the land surfaces.

Several plains states contain badlands—North and South Dakota, Wyoming, Kansas, and Nebraska. Badlands also occur in other parts of the United States and the world, but the badlands in those places are not as dramatic as those in South Dakota.

A more detailed and complete definition of the word badlands fits only one place—the southwest region of South Dakota. There is found the best, most extensive, and most spectacular example of badlands. Some of South Dakota's badland gullies cut as deep as 500 feet into the Earth, while some cliffs and spires rise hundreds of feet above the area's rivers. There are thousands of square miles of rock formations, and the variety and color

The Palisades

of the rocks with which nature has endowed this corner of the world is stunning. The formations create seemingly endless expanses of strange and desolate, but colorful and breathtaking, land sculptures.

So unusual is this place of scenic and geologic wealth that the United States Congress authorized a National Monument as far back as 1929. In 1978, Congress made the area a full-fledged National Park—Badlands National Park—recognizing the unique value of the place to present and future generations.

Badlands National Park covers an area of 244,000 acres. That is about one-third the size of the state of Rhode Island.

How did this remarkable place in South Dakota come to be?

2

Birth of the Badlands

The story of the Badlands began more than 100 million years ago. At that time, a huge sea covered the area where the Badlands now stand. As the land rose, much of the water drained away. What remained was a shallow saltwater sea that scientists have called the Pierre (pronounced PEER) Sea. This great shallow sea extended from Canada to the Gulf of Mexico.

About 65 to 80 million years ago, underground flows of molten rock produced great upheavals in the Earth. The upheavals caused the future Black Hills of South Dakota to rise. The Black Hills, to the west of the Badlands, are rugged mountains that tower above the surrounding plains. The hills got their name from their heavily forested slopes, which are so dark they appear black from afar.

The pushing and folding of the Earth's surface also created the western mountains that would later be called the Rockies. The large saltwater sea, too, was affected by those violent forces churning inside the Earth. The upheaval caused the land under the sea to rise, and the sea's water to drain away.

Formations show erosion. At Dillon Pass you can see the different rock layers.

The newly exposed seabed was a layer of dark mud, or sediment, that had been collecting for millions of years. As the sediment dried, it formed a layer of shale that came to be called Pierre Shale. It forms the deepest and oldest layer of the Badlands region. Up to 2,000 feet thick, the shale contains fossils of sea lizards, giant sea turtles, plesiosaurs, fish, and other marine animals that had lived in the ancient saltwater sea.

About 37 million years ago, streams from the western hills and mountains began carrying sand and gravel to the lowland, the former seabed. The streams and the many layers of sediment that the streams carried began creating a marshy plain on top of the Pierre Shale. Later, volcanoes to the west ejected huge volumes of ash that were carried by winds and water. The ash settled on top of the already numerous layers of sediment that had been deposited on the marshy plain. As each layer of sediment was deposited, the layer beneath it hardened and turned to rock. The layers were of varying hardness and thickness, and of different colors: yellow, red, silvery gray, tan. These layers of sediment and ash that washed across and settled on the Pierre Shale grew to be hundreds of feet deep.

Scientists have given the name *Oligocene Epoch* to the period of history during which the many layers of sediment and ash were deposited on the marshy plains. Lasting about 11 million years, the Oligocene was the period of time from 34 million to 23 million years ago.

During the Oligocene, wildlife flourished on the warm, marshy plain. Three-toed horses and camels—no bigger than a medium-sized dog of today; giant pigs; saber-toothed tigers; and a large rhinoceroslike beast called the titanothere, meaning "Titan-beast," were but a few of the numerous species of mammals that thrived. These mammals had come gradually to replace the dinosaurs, which had become extinct millions of years before. Some of the

Oligocene mammals were the ancestors of many of the animals we know today.

Trees, flowering plants, and other lush vegetation also were abundant in the warm, moist, subtropical climate of the Oligocene Epoch.

As the animals of the Oligocene died, their remains were buried by periodic floods and the continuing deposits of layers of sediment. Other animals just sank into the ooze and decaying vegetation of the marshes. Many fossils of the animals and plants of that epoch are still being discovered today in the Badlands. It is because of these remarkable finds of mammal fossils in the Badlands that the Oligocene came to be known as the "Golden Age of Mammals."

As the Oligocene Epoch approached its end, the climate became drier and cooler. Grasslands, able to survive with less water, replaced the swampy marshes and forests. The animals changed too. Species of grass-eating animals began to enter the area, as the marsh-dwelling species disappeared along with the marshes. As the climate became cooler, more vigorous animals began replacing those that had thrived only in the earlier subtropical climate.

Colorful peaks rise up from the prairie.

When rain came to some of these drier grasslands, it was heavy, but it didn't last long. With such downpours, streams swelled quickly and eroded the fragile layers of earth, eventually creating deep gullies, steep small hills, and the unusual shapes of the Badlands formations. Because the layers of rock in the Badlands are of varying depths and hardness, they erode at different rates and in different shapes.

This variation in weathering helps create the amazing rough landscape of the Badlands—buttes, ridges, canyons, as well as natural bridges, arches, and other unusual formations. The Badlands' layers of rock are like a chart of geologic history, to be read from the bottom layer of shale up to the top layers that were added during later years of geologic history.

The process of erosion in the Badlands continues to this day. Water, wind, and ice carve away an average of one inch of stone and soil each year. Some soft material erodes several inches a year, while harder, more resistant material may take centuries to erode even an inch.

Because the average rate of erosion in the Badlands is one of the highest known, the face of the Badlands is never the same. It is constantly being carved into new configurations. If the rate of erosion remains the same, some scientists believe that the Badlands will be transformed into a flat prairie in half a million years.

The sediments that are being eroded from the Badlands are washed away by the White, Bad, and Cheyenne Rivers—the three main rivers in the Badlands area. Eventually, the sediments are deposited in the Gulf of Mexico by way of the Missouri and Mississippi Rivers. Thus continues the worldwide cycle of erosion and deposition, the carrying of sediments from one place to another. Thus continues the process that created the Badlands and that still shapes its ever-changing landscape.

3
Early Inhabitants of the Badlands

Though the Badlands began forming millions of years ago, scientists believe that human beings have lived in the region for fewer than 12,000 years. Little is known about these early inhabitants, but fragments of their pottery and tools have been found in archeological excavations—digs made in search of items from long ago. The charcoal remains of these early people's campfires have also been found and tested by a scientific process called carbon dating. The process determines accurately the age of ancient objects. Evaluating the charcoal, scientists have determined that it—and its users—go back nearly 12,000 years.

These earliest-known Badlands inhabitants hunted the Colombian mammoth, a huge animal that existed at the time. Its meat provided food and its fur was the source of clothing. The mammoth was so huge it could be hunted safely only if it became trapped in deep mud. Once the thick mud trapped the animal, the people could slay it with spears.

As the mammoth became extinct, a species of bison came into being. Bison is the name scientists use for the animal commonly known as the buffalo. The early buffalo was much larger than the buffalo we see today. Weighing about 6,000 pounds, these early animals, like the mammoths, were too large for people to kill with spears alone. To hunt them, people devised a method of stampeding the buffalo over the edge of cliffs, causing the animals to fall to their death. The animals were then prepared for use as food and clothing.

About 1,000 years ago, tribes of nomadic, or wandering, native people lived in the Badlands. By 1750, the area was dominated by the Sioux Indians. *Sioux* is the name white people gave to the natives who lived throughout the northern plains. There were several groups within this large native tribe. Those living in the western Dakotas and Nebraska called themselves Lakota, which means "allies" or "friends."

Sioux culture—Lakota culture—was based largely on buffalo hunting. Native families used buffalo meat for food; buffalo hides for clothing and housing—tepee making; and buffalo bones to make tools. For hunting, the Sioux used horses, introduced to the New World by early Spanish colonizers. With horses, the Sioux could hunt buffalo easily. Their culture flourished as millions of buffalo roamed the plains, for that was the time of the great

This woman is preparing a buffalo hide on a stretched frame.

buffalo herds. Some herds were so huge that they darkened huge sections of the plains. Herds were measured not in numbers, but in the area they covered. One herd in 1839 measured 30 by 45 miles. That's an area larger than the state of Rhode Island.

Among the first white travelers through the Badlands were members of the Lewis and Clark Expedition, which set out for the West in 1803. Meriwether Lewis, a former Army officer and a friend of President Thomas Jefferson, was chosen to head the search for a land route to the

Pacific Ocean. All along the way, Lewis sent scouts ahead to explore possible directions to take. Such scouts were sent to the Badlands area too. Their report of the place's harsh terrain and lack of water persuaded the expedition leaders to take another route across the plains.

Jedediah Strong Smith and his party of 13 fur trappers fared no better in the Badlands when they traveled through in 1823. Smith was an explorer whose life was spent in unusually wide and adventurous travels. Nonetheless, it was the Badlands that nearly did him and his party in. They nearly died for lack of water until, desperate, they finally happened to stumble upon a spring. Before the water was found, two of Smith's men became so exhausted and dehydrated that Smith buried them with only their heads showing to keep their bodies cool and thus save their lives.

Though the Badlands have been fascinating to all people who ever passed through them, the area has always offered special challenges to travelers.

4

Native People, Cowboys, and Homesteaders

As the United States grew and the frontier began to open up, the expansion of railroads west of the Mississippi had a great impact on the plains. In the late 1850s and the 1860s, as tracks were put down ever westward, thousands of workers invaded the territory. Workers needed to be fed, and the plentiful buffalo in the area became their major food supply. Hunters were employed to slaughter enough buffalo to feed the work crews. The native inhabitants of the plains did not object to white peoples' killing of buffalo for food, but such reasonable slaughter of the animal did not last. Buffalo hunting soon became a popular if senseless sport.

For $25, a hunter could take a special train excursion into buffalo country and shoot as many buffalo as his skill allowed. One hunter could kill as many as 500 animals in one day, and usually, only the hide and tongue of the buffalo were taken as trophies. The rest of the animal was left to rot in the sun. This thoughtless slaughter of the buffalo became a major source of conflict between Native Americans and white people. Because the buffalo was the main source of life for the plains natives,

A woman is cooking in front of a tipi. She has placed corn on high racks so it will dry in the sun.

they could not allow such large numbers of the animal to be carelessly wasted.

Other conflicts also arose between native people and the white newcomers. As the U.S. Army, homesteaders, and gold miners began moving West, their presence and growing numbers increasingly interfered with the simple relationship that the natives wished to keep with nature. Natives frequently clashed with white people, and resisted being settled on reservations, a practice that became more common as white people took over more land. The Sioux struggled long and hard to maintain their independence, but after years of conflict, their way of life at last came to an end with the Massacre of Wounded Knee. In 1890, meeting with continued Sioux resistance, federal troops trapped and killed more than 200 Sioux men, women, and children at Wounded Knee, which is located

Round-up on the Dakota prairies.

about 25 miles south of the Badlands. It was the last major confrontation between Native Americans and white people.

By 1890, fewer than 1,000 buffalo survived of the estimated 60 million that had once roamed the prairie. With the buffalo near extinction, millions of acres of prairie grasslands became available for cattle grazing. At the same time, with the Native Americans pushed onto reservations, no obstacles existed to white people's use of the land. The door was opened for cattle grazing and for the era of the American cowboy.

Texans and other western cattlemen sent their herds to the plains to be fattened up for market. The grazing herds were tended by cowboys, many of whom were quite young—from 17 to 21 years of age. Cowboys controlled herds that typically numbered about 2,000 head of cattle.

These young men spent 16 or 17 hours a day in the saddle, driving the cattle to pasture and water, protecting them from wild animals and thieves, branding them at periodic roundups, and driving them finally to shipping points from which they would go to market. A cowboy's greatest fear was a stampede, a wild rush of the herd. A stampede sometimes was brought on by the cattles' fear of stormy weather or by a sudden fright. Cowboys often sang mournful ballads to the herds. The soothing melodies calmed the restless cattle.

Most cowboys earned a dollar a day. Though the work was adventurous and free-spirited, it was also difficult, lonely, and harsh. Cowboys usually worked no more than seven years.

By the late 1800s, the cowboy era came to an end. Persistent snow and late spring storms killed many of the cattle, ending the great cattle drives. After that, herds would be raised on ranches, and the many acres of open prairie, once the fenceless empires of cattlemen, would be open for the next wave of prairie newcomers—the homesteaders.

Homesteaders were farmers who acquired land on the prairie under the terms of the Homestead Act. A homestead is a small farm. The act, passed by Congress in

Each year the cowboys branded all the calves.

1862, transferred 160 acres of land, essentially free of charge, to any farmer who agreed to settle on it and to work it for five years according to some general requirements. It was an offer that took off like wildfire. Thousands of people from the United States as well as immigrants from many European countries poured onto the prairie. The earliest homesteaders settled in Minnesota, Kansas, and Nebraska, but in the 1880s, the Dakota Territory attracted the most land seekers. By 1890, the area that is now South Dakota had a population of about 350,000. Twenty years earlier, its population had been less than 12,000. But if the offer of a free farm was appealing, homesteading often was painfully difficult.

5

Homestead Life

The vast, flat, grassy, and treeless prairie offered abundant land to be fenced in by eager farmers, but life on prairie farms presented endless challenges. Because there were few trees on the prairie, many of the early farmers had to use sod to build huts to live in. Sod is a piece of earth with grass growing on it. The homesteaders cut sod by digging 3 inches into the earth while tracing an oblong shape about 6 inches across and 14 inches long. The piece of sod was then lifted out of the ground and stacked piece on top of piece to form the walls of a hut. Such sod structures were generally small—about 12 by 24 feet. It was not until years later that trains brought lumber to the prairie for housebuilding.

A sod house, called a soddy, often provided only scant protection. Winter snow sometimes blew in though chinks in the sod walls, and sod roofs often leaked during rainstorms. A sod roof could look quaint in the summer as the grass greened and wildflowers bloomed in its midst.

Daily life on a homestead was an endless routine of hard work. Women hauled water, sometimes over long distances, and they gathered dried buffalo droppings,

This sod house probably served as both home to the teacher and school to children who lived within a few miles.

MARY CLARK, teacher at Maass school – 1908

called "buffalo chips," to burn as fuel for heat and cooking. They washed clothes by hand on rough-surfaced washboards, and collected grease to make soap and candles. Food for the winter months had to be prepared and stored in the ground in shelters called root cellars. From an early age, children helped with all the indoor and outdoor chores.

Men along with the women and children had to endure backbreaking work in the fields. Even so, they could never be sure of a successful harvest. Violent thunderstorms and hail, characteristic of prairie climate, could destroy an entire crop in a few minutes. Sometimes, hail stones as large as baseballs fell, breaking windows and injuring farm animals. Lightning often set dry grassy fields on fire. When a drought occurred, crops did not grow at all, but even if they did, sometimes swarms of grasshoppers invaded the fields and ate the plants.

Winter on the vast open prairie was especially fierce. Blizzards sometimes isolated homesteaders for weeks at a time. So blinding were the blizzards that farmers often tied a line from their soddy to their barn. The line helped guide the farmer back to the house after he took care of the animals.

After a series of severe winters and unproductive summers, many homesteaders gave up and simply walked away from their farms when spring came. Some of the buildings they abandoned still dot the prairie landscape.

If homesteading was filled with so many hardships, were there any satisfactions? The homesteaders who stayed took pleasure in owning their own farms. They got a feeling of accomplishment in meeting the challenges of nature. And, as towns arose and more farmers settled, neighbors helped each other and provided a greater social life. A sense of humor mixed in with the hardships and heavy work helped many a farmer through the difficult times. One homesteader who settled just north of the Badlands good-naturedly wrote the story, many years later, of the prairie winters he spent there. This homesteader was a bachelor, a number of whom took up homesteading alone in hopes of getting established on land of their own. To help keep heat inside his shanty, he had lined it with tar paper and then piled sod high around the foundation. His mattress was a sack stuffed with buffalo grass.

This homesteader described his winter bedtime routine in this way: "I would stay up late and keep a roaring fire....The teakettle would be boiling, the room nice and cozy. I would pull my bed down, keep on some of my heavy underwear, wrap some wool comforters around me, and lie down on the buffalo-grass mattress. No lights, no radio, no TV, no company, no conversation, no reading, nothing. I just wrapped up and retired. By morning the water in the teakettle would be a solid chunk of ice, and I soon learned that the only way I could keep my supply of potatoes from freezing was to leave them behind the stove during the daytime, and take them to bed with me at night. Potatoes don't make the most comfortable bed companions!"

Farmers on the prairie today may keep their potatoes in bins instead of their beds, but they still have to work hard to run their farms. Water remains scarce and a valuable commodity in many places, although deep wells are dug so that water no longer has to be carried from streams. And today, with telephones, automobiles, and other modern means of communication, farmers can get together easily. They can cooperate on projects to prevent and overcome the effects of drought and storms.

The Sioux are still a strong force in the Badlands area, especially on the Pine Ridge Indian Reservation, part of which lies within Badlands National Park. There they graze cattle, and join with other ranchers on the surrounding prairie to cooperate in neighborly ways. In the spring, when it's time to brand calves, the neighbors help each other, going from ranch to ranch until all the branding is finished. And what all of the inhabitants of the region share in common is a love of the Badlands area, with its majestic and haunting beauty, and its special peacefulness.

6

Plants, Birds, and Other Animals of the Badlands

At first glance, a visitor might get the impression that the Badlands cannot support living things. The severe landscape does not appear friendly to plants and animals. Yet, many species of plants and animals make their home on the grassy prairies and the rocky cliffs of Badlands National Park.

The park, containing one of the last stretches of wild prairie in the United States, has more than 40 species of grass. America's natural prairie was nearly destroyed by the people who settled on the land and turned it into croplands, and built towns, cities, and roads. Many of the grasses in the Badlands, however, have been restored by the National Park Service.

More than grasses grow in Badlands National Park. From early spring to late fall, approximately 200 species of wildflowers add dots of color to the prairie landscape.

Early in the spring, prairie violets and white or bluish hood phlox begin to bloom. Patches of vetches and loco-weed also cover the land with their purple, blue, or red blossoms. Locoweed got that name because, when eaten

29

Sheep Mountain Table Area

by livestock, it can make the animals behave in a confused way. *Loco* means "crazy" in Spanish.

As the season moves on, salsify, prairie coneflowers, tufted evening-primrose, and scarlet globemallow are but a few of the flowers that appear. The Sioux used the yellow coneflower to make a tealike beverage, and salsify to make medicine. In summer, the bluish flowers of the Indian turnip blooms too. At one time, the Sioux harvested the turniplike root of the plant for use as a vegetable.

With autumn, blazingstar and prairie aster come to life. Blazingstar, too, once was used as a medicine to treat fever.

A variety of shrubs and trees share parts of the Badlands landscape. In the drier areas, the vegetation ranges from sagebrush to cactus. In the moister, more sheltered regions, juniper, slippery elm, cottonwood, skunkbush sumac, and wild rose are established.

The grasses, flowers, shrubs, and trees all support a surprisingly large variety of wildlife. More than 30 different mammals live in the Badlands. Probably the most awesome is the buffalo. The animal was nearly brought to extinction in the 19th century by hunters. In 1963, however, buffalo were successfully reintroduced to the Badlands by the National Park Service, as part of its project to restore the vanishing prairie. Today, more than 400 buffalo graze in the Sage Creek Wilderness Area, a large grasslands area located in the northern section of the park.

Seeing buffalo is exciting, but it is important to remember that they are wild animals and can be dangerous if approached too closely. A large buffalo bull can weigh as much as a small car, and can run faster than a horse. Buffalo also can be cantankerous and unpredictable. Bulls are especially aggressive during the summer breeding season, and a buffalo cow is mighty protective of her calf. She'll respond aggressively if approached or in any way threatened or antagonized.

Another erosion showcase.

One of the most delightful creatures in the Badlands is the blacktail prairie dog. It resembles its relative, the groundhog. Though round and short-legged, the prairie dog moves surprisingly quickly with an amusing kind of waddling scamper. In between sleeping, eating, tending to its young, and keeping watch for predators, this highly social animal finds plenty of time to spend with fellow prairie dogs. They are often seen grooming and caressing each other, and sometimes touch mouths as if they were kissing. Prairie dogs communicate with each other by a number of different calls or barks. When a prairie dog barks at you, it is telling its fellows that danger is near.

American bison, better known as buffalo

The animal got the dog part of its name because of its puppylike bark.

Prairie dogs live in colonies called towns. The towns, in turn, are divided into wards. Within a ward, each prairie dog family has its own territory. Prairie dogs dig burrows for refuge from predators and the extremes of weather. Grass and some weeds make up the bulk of their diet. There are many prairie dog towns in Badlands National Park, but they are not easily seen from the road. Roberts Prairie Dog Town, located on Sage Creek Rim Road not far from the town of Pinnacles, is an excellent

Prairie dogs

place to watch the antics of these active and amusing rodents.

Buffalo like to visit prairie dog towns too. The loose dirt in the mounds around the burrows provides ideal wallowing sites for dust baths. Coating its hide with dust helps protect a buffalo from pestering insects.

Another animal that inhabits the Badlands is the pronghorn, often called antelope. Pronghorns are most often seen on the upper prairie of the Badlands or in the Sage Creek Wilderness Area. Adult pronghorns depend on their sharp eyesight and great speed to detect and

Pronghorn antelope   *Young mule deer*

avoid enemies. The fastest animal in North America, the pronghorn can reach speeds of 50 to 60 miles an hour. A young pronghorn, called a kid, uses a different strategy for protection. The kid remains motionless while lying pressed against the earth. So well does its color blend with the earth that you can walk as close as three feet away from it and not see the animal!

Mule deer and whitetail deer are also present in the park, although mule deer are more common. How can you tell them apart? The whitetail runs with its tail up, as if the tail were a flag flying. The mule deer has a black-tipped tail which it doesn't hold up while running. And mule deer have larger ears than the whitetail.

The Badlands were originally inhabited by Audubon bighorn sheep, but they were hunted to extinction by 1920. In 1964, the National Park Service released Rocky Mountain bighorn sheep into the park. These bighorns are close relatives to the extinct Audubon bighorns. The rugged Badlands terrain provides a suitable home for the bighorn, which rely on their superior climbing ability in rough country to escape predators.

The coyote, though long persecuted by people for being a threat to livestock, is expanding its range. Coyotes eat anything from prairie dogs and mice to the fruits of the pricklypear cactus. Campers in the Badlands often hear an evening serenade by the coyotes. It's an eerie song you'll not soon forget. If you drive through the park at night, you may see a coyote's yellow eyes peering out at you from the side of the road. Coyotes are largely nocturnal—they come out at night—but they also can be seen by day.

Other animals are present in the Badlands on a smaller scale. Chipmunks, jackrabbits, badgers, bobcats, mountain lions, bats, porcupines, desert cottontail rabbits, and a variety of reptiles and amphibians—frogs, toads, and salamanders—also roam the area.

Rocky Mountain bighorn sheep

Desert cottontail fluffed up to keep warm

Chipmunks are often seen on the buttes, but their coloring blends in with the background. Such camouflage protects the chipmunk from hawks, eagles, and other predators, but it also can make them hard to spot by people.

Jackrabbits actually are hares rather than rabbits. Hares are larger than rabbits. Jackrabbits are noted for their fast speed and long ears, but you might not get to see any. They are nocturnal creatures. Visitors have better luck spotting the desert cottontail. Smaller than the jackrabbit, the cottontail is fairly common and does not hide during the day.

The bobcat got its name from its short bobtail. It, too, is basically nocturnal, so you're not likely to spot one unless you're camping at night in an area where one happens to be.

The badger is powerfully built with long claws for digging. This plump animal might be seen trying to pull some dinner—a prairie dog—from its burrow.

In the Badlands, mammals are joined by more than 120 species of birds. Some are permanent residents, while others migrate south for the winter. Often, the birds are found in areas where there are some trees and shrubs nearby to provide shelter.

The western meadowlark, with a black V on its yellow breast, is easy to spot by either its color or song. It nests on the ground in dense grasses, but often flies to a higher perch to fill the air with its loud and melodious, flutelike song.

The black and white magpie with its long tail is striking to see and easy to spot. This is a bold and dramatic bird whose song, too, is bold and noticeable—a series of loud, harsh notes.

White-throated swifts and cliff swallows find the cliff faces in the Badlands fine for nesting. When the swallows fly south for the winter, rosy finches often move into the swallows' mud nests for the cold months. The cliffs provide homes for other birds too. Rock wrens build nests in cliff crevasses, and mountain bluebirds also commonly nest in cliff cavities.

Grackles, grouse, killdeer, and hawks are often seen, and an occasional pair of golden eagles, with their majestic seven-foot wingspread, have also been known to rear their young on the high buttes of the Badlands.

There is also life to be found rippling along the ground in search of prey. Bullsnakes, yellow-bellied racers, and prairie rattlesnakes live in the Badlands, though these shy creatures often "freeze" or flee from people before being spotted. Be cautious about rattlesnakes. If provoked, these animals will bite and release a poison called venom. A person who is bitten should be treated by a doctor as soon as possible.

All wildlife in the Badlands is protected—animals may not be hunted or taken. Such protection saves the animals for future generations to enjoy.

Seeing examples of its wildlife adds great interest to a visit to the Badlands. Be sure to bring binoculars to close in on animals that may be far away in this big park.

7
A Visit to the Badlands

As you make your way through the Badlands, the startling rock formations have a way of springing up on you all at once, just about taking your breath away. Suddenly, there they are, some rising sharply skyward, others creating great vistas below eye level. And right along with the marvelous stone outcroppings carved by nature are the prairie grasslands. Some grassy areas are large, some small; some located high, some low; some as flat as tabletops, some rolling gently. The unpredictable Badlands landscape is full of wonderful surprises.

There are many ways to explore the Badlands. After entering the park, it's a good idea to stop at one of the two visitor centers: Cedar Pass Visitor Center or the White River Visitor Center. Park guides and a variety of exhibits and materials are there to acquaint you with the area and prepare you for your stay. You can also buy books and maps at the visitor centers. There's a lot to see in the Badlands and the terrain can be rugged so you want to be sure to plan your visit wisely.

Many miles of roads–some hardtop, some unpaved–go through the park, with wayside exhibits and signs along

Chimney Butte

Erosion has cut deep gullies throughout the Badlands.

the routes that point out areas of interest. Avoid the unpaved roads without first checking with a park guide.

Throughout the summer, demonstrations about fossils, a variety of slide talks, star programs, and night hikes are scheduled. Several self-guiding nature trails also have been mapped out. They're short in length but provide a great deal to see and learn.

One of the self-guiding trails is the Door Trail. It starts in a opening, a "door," through some Badlands rock formations. Go through the door to the trail that leads into one of the most rugged areas of the Badlands. Along the trail are clues to understanding how the remarkable landforms were created through ages of erosion. The trail is three-quarters of a mile long round trip

Fossil Exhibit Trail

A summer storm over the Badlands

and takes only about 45 minutes, but the views are astonishing. You'll see gullies so deep that shadows hide the bottom. You'll also see armored mudballs! They're balls of mud over which a coating of stones became embedded as the balls rolled down streams.

The Fossil Exhibit Trail is only one-quarter of a mile long, but it gives a good geologic history of the Badlands, and it's a great place to begin to understand the remarkable fossils that have made the Badlands famous.

The Cliff Shelf Trail takes you to Cliff Shelf, which was formed when a huge block of stone broke loose from a cliff and fell to the ground. The chunk of stone, weighing thousands of tons, must have come down with quite a crash; it compacted significantly when it hit the ground. A small pond on the shelf keeps refilling during the rainy spring and early summer months, creating a home for a great variety of plants and animals. You'll see juniper and cottonwood trees and cattails, and a wide assortment of animals and birds in this Badlands oasis. An oasis is a small, fertile, water-filled area in the midst of dry land.

There are also guided nature walks led regularly by park naturalists. For an even deeper understanding of the Badlands, backpacking is an excellent idea. The 64,000 acres of roadless land that is designated the Sage Creek Wilderness Area is ideal for backpacking. Hiking, horseback riding, and camping also are permitted throughout the park with few restrictions, but be sure to heed them. Absolutely no campfires are allowed within the park because of the fire danger to prairie grasslands. No rocks, wildlife, fossils, or other materials may be removed, and remember to take fresh water with you when you're hiking or camping. The water in the creeks and canyons is not suitable for drinking.

If you're not up to camping, you can rent a cabin—be sure to get a reservation first—at the Cedar Pass Lodge, next to the visitors center. The lodge has a shop where you can buy beautiful Sioux jewelry and crafts, as well as other gifts and souvenirs.

One place in the park that's especially rich in wildlife and provides a panoramic view of a large section of the

Badlands is the Sage Creek Wilderness Area. Located in the northern part of the park, the area is home to the park's buffalo and many other animals. Drive along Sage Creek Rim Road or go hiking or backpacking in the Sage Creek Area.

A few miles down Sage Creek Rim Road is Roberts Prairie Dog Town. There, the furry inhabitants are sure to entertain you.

The southern part of the park, acquired in 1976, contains part of the Pine Ridge Indian Reservation. The terrain is rugged so be sure to check with a park ranger before heading there. The area features spectacular examples of badlands as well as many sites of historic and religious significance to the Sioux. The area contains numerous tables of many sizes. The tables, as they are called, are areas of land that are virtually flat on top and often heavily grassed. Some are only a few feet across; others are hundreds of acres. They are surrounded completely by steep drop-offs on all sides. Religious activities on one of these tables helped trigger the confrontation of Sioux and federal troops at Wounded Knee.

After seeing an outstanding stretch of prairie in Badlands National Park, you might enjoy seeing a prairie homestead. There's just such a homestead—the Prairie Homestead Historic Site—near the eastern entrance to

Evening splendor in the Badlands

A pot of gold at the base of a rainbow seems possible in the beautiful Badlands of South Dakota.

the park. It's a restored sod and log dwelling that homesteaders of the early 1900s built on the site. Furnished as if the homestead family were living there today, it's the only original sod dwelling on public display in South Dakota.

Weather in the Badlands can be an adventure in itself. It can be quite changeable from one day to the next. Summer is usually sunny with highs in the 90s. A few days may top 100° Fahrenheit. Nighttime temperatures can drop as low as 55° Fahrenheit, but the extremes usually are not so great. Summer heat often causes quivering mirages across the Badlands landforms, adding even greater mystery to the landscape. Thunderstorms can bring high winds, hail, and lightning. It is fascinating to watch lightning over the Badlands at night. The display can be seen from many miles away.

Autumn has mild and pleasant days, but snow can fall in late September. The crisp, clear days of early autumn—before the heavy snows fly—is an especially comfortable time in the Badlands.

Winter days can sometimes be mild under the influence of a chinook, a warm, dry wind that sometimes descends from the eastern side of the Rockies. But snow also falls frequently, and sometimes there are blizzards with howling winds and temperatures that can plunge lower than 20° below zero Fahrenheit.

Spring is a beautiful time to visit the Badlands. That's when many of the wildflowers are in bloom, and the weather is pleasant. Warming begins in March, though blizzards are possible through April. But whatever the time of year you visit, the Badlands are sure to show you many memorable sides of its everchanging face.

If you have time, there are many beautiful places—far too numerous to mention here—to visit in the area around the Badlands. Many of these sites are no more than two to four hours away. The famous Black Hills are just 50 miles west of the park. Custer State Park, a part of the Black Hills, is the second largest state park in the United States. It includes a large herd of buffalo.

While you're in the area of Custer, drive the short distance to Mt. Rushmore, the massive monument that honors Presidents Washington, Jefferson, Lincoln, and Theodore Roosevelt. The four presidents' faces are carved into a mountainside. Each face is 60 feet tall! It took 14 years to complete the sculpture.

Jewel Cavern National Monument, also in the area, is the world's fourth longest cave. And if you have time to travel 535 miles from the Badlands, you can see Wyoming's Yellowstone National Park. There you'll see "Old Faithful" and other natural wonders. Call Yellowstone first to check road and weather conditions.

More than 1,300,000 people visit the Badlands each year. With good reason. The Badlands, millions of years old, are an everchanging work of natural sculpture. Rich in remarkable scenery and geologic history, it is also a place of wonder and haunting mystery. Even the Badlands wind, rustling up arid gulches and across prairie grasses, can play havoc with sound. Is it the whining wind that you hear, or a child sobbing? Or ancient natives whispering chants, or perhaps the cry of long-gone buffalo wolves echoing back across the ages. All around, the Badlands are a feast for endless imagination.

Index